Santa's 911 Meeting

Author Genie Byrd

Illustrator Margaret Caudle

Xulon PRESS

Santa's 911 Meeting
by Author Genie Byrd Illustrator Margaret Caudle

Printed in the United States of America

ISBN 9781628396478

www.xulonpress.com

Author's preface

Authors cannot claim the position without carefully considering how we got to that place.

I've dreamed of writing children's books for as long as I can remember. Important "real life" issues claimed first priority, including marriage, family, educational pursuits, teaching, playing the organ at church and helping those in need! Finally, I can now focus on writing, the love I've had to leave behind!

I could not have accomplished this goal without the devotion, encouragement, assistance and love from James, my husband and my "Bud." Thank you sweetheart, from way down deep!

My sister-in-law, Gale Ard is, without doubt, one of my best friends. She has listened with empathy, provided editing suggestions when asked, and been a consistent encourager. I love you, Gale, and I am greatly indebted to you.

Finding an illustrator who could paint my visions for Santa's 911 Meeting was a challenge. Excellent, experienced illustrators abound, yet what I needed most was someone who knew me well and would hear my heart in pictures. During this search, my mind went to Margaret Caudle, a multi-talented teacher at Addison Elementary, where I retired as school principal. Margaret painted unbelievable murals, which continue to give pleasure to the Addison school family and community. I was delighted when Margaret agreed to illustrate Santa's 911 Meeting, and even more for the product of her artistic genius!

Jose Medina, from Xulon Press, has been a blessing night and day. I've asked hundreds of sometimes nutty, laughable questions. His patience, guidance and knowledge have helped me get through the enormous steps to publication. Thanks, Jose, for believing I could!

Thanks to my family who continued to ask where I was in this process and encouraged me to keep pressing on to completion.

Santa's 911 Meeting is dedicated to my grandson, Ellis Byrd. He is a wonderful son, brother, grandson, student and creative writer, in his own right.

Ellis' fun with, "what if," provided just the needed spark to launch my long awaited desire to write children's books. Thank you, Ellis. We will read your books one day.

Tap . . . tap . . . tap . . . tap . . . tap

The elves' hammers stop suddenly, as Santa's voice booms over a speaker. Elves and all of Toyland know to stop and listen when Santa speaks.

"Everyone come to the Toyland Auditorium at five-thirty for a 911 meeting. That means everyone!"

Whispers fly fast among the elves in Toyland:
"What do you think has happened?"
"Is he going to announce a bonus for us?"
"Perhaps I am being chosen for something special!"

Everyone knows Santa only calls a 911 meeting when something very important happens.

Each elf has a different thought about the reason for the meeting. So many possibilities! Ears perk up and listen to the village clock tick- tock as five-thirty nears.

Toyland's mayor, police chief, teachers, elf moms and dads, brothers and sisters, cousins, and friends crowd into the huge auditorium. Many of the reindeer that work for Santa are already seated, anxiously awaiting Santa's arrival.

A cheer breaks out as Santa and Mrs. Claus walk on to the stage. Santa picks up the microphone, holds up his hand for everyone to be quiet, and begins to speak.

"Faithful citizens of Toyland, when I call a 911 meeting, it is because something is really wrong. I've called you together this afternoon because I need your help."

Everyone listened, wide-eyed.
"As you know, many of our reindeer have been sick with the dreaded reindeer flu.

"I'm happy to say some are better. But I'm sad to say many of our reindeer are still on the sick list: Dasher, Dancer, Prancer, and Vixen. Comet, Cupid, Donder, and Blixen are still sick, too and I'm so sorry to report, Rudolph is still running a high fever."

A gasp is heard from the audience. Anxious voices whisper, "No! Not them... it can't be! What will we do?"

Santa's voice is calm, yet firm. "I need you to help me choose a new team to pull my sleigh. You know each other well in Toyland, and you know who will be the very best for this huge task of delivering Christmas toys around the world."

Reindeer eyes flash with importance. They look at each other and at the hundreds of elves and animals who would make the big decision.

"Please remember the team must be very special, with leadership skills I can depend on," adds Santa. "Who do you recommend?"

Elf Ellis is seated on the back row. He isn't sure Santa can hear him, but he speaks his loudest and gives it a try. "Santa, Santa, I nominate Reindeer Maurice. He speaks many languages, and has a kind heart."

Santa nods approval at Elf Ellis, a talented elf with red hair.

Mrs. Claus types Reindeer Maurice's name on her computer. Suddenly, on a large screen in front of the room, everyone can see Maurice's name.

"I nominate Reindeer Jin," says Elf Jacob. "He never gets tired or slows down. He volunteers to pull sleighs full of groceries for older elves and reindeer. He is strong and kind. We need a leader with his kind of work ethic."

Reindeer Jin's name appears on the screen.

Elf Caroline remembers how Marcelles helped everyone stay calm when the lights went out during a big snowstorm. "I nominate Reindeer Marcelles. We need a leader that helps others and stays calm in a crisis."

Everyone nods and Marcelles' name appears on the list.

"We need someone that can solve problems!" adds Elf Reagan. "The best problem solver in Toyland is Reindeer Joon! Elves and reindeer of all ages visit him when they have problems. He really cares and listens carefully. Reindeer Joon is my nominee."

Mrs. Claus adds Reindeer Joon's name to the list of reindeer nominated for the team.

"I nominate Reindeer Claudia," shouts Jonas! She always tells the truth and is friendly to everyone. Reindeer Claudia teaches the young elves and reindeer the importance of being honest. We need a leader that tells the truth and is loyal."

"Good work, so far," said Santa.

"We also, need a quick thinker. This team has to be determined and dedicated to getting the job done. There are many things to remember when we're up in the sky. It's hard work, so no slackers!"

Heads nod and a few giggles are heard.

Elf Nathan jumps to his feet. "Oh, I know a reindeer that worked many extra hours doing the work for those who have been sick. I nominate Reindeer Juan Pablo for the team. He's no slacker!"

Reindeer Juan Pablo gives Elf Nathan a big smile.

Maurice
Jin
Ma...lles
...n...dia
Juan Pablo

Mrs. Claus adds Reindeer Juan Pablo's name. She counts the reindeer nominated. "That gives us six names to consider. We need three more names."

"Reindeer Malan is very strong and always happy," suggests Elf Jessica. "The very cold weather in his homeland of Greenland never gets him down. He takes each day as it comes and does his best. He will be great for the team."

"I have an idea," chimes Elf Jarrod. "We need someone who is good in math. Reindeer Reyha is a great mathematician. She will be great counting all those presents."

So, Reindeer Malan and Reindeer Reyha go on the list, bringing the number to eight.

"Yay! We're almost finished. We have chosen our team," shouts Elf Alex.

Everyone claps and cheers, knowing they are doing a great job.

"Not so fast, dear Toyland citizens," says Santa calmly. "Who will fill in for Rudolph? This reindeer must have all of the leadership qualities you've named to fill Reindeer Rudolph's job. We must also remember, a reindeer's nose is very important."

Maurice
Jin
Marcelles
Joon
Claudia
Juan Pablo
Malan
Reyha

A quiet hush falls over the big auditorium, as everyone is deep in thought.

Then Mayor Moose stands to speak.

"You know each other well; that's true. You have chosen the team carefully. To those names I would like to nominate a reindeer we all love and trust.

"She's dedicated to Toyland and always does her personal best in any job she is given. She follows the rules and comforts the sad and lonely with kind words and deeds.

"She also listens well and helps us agree when we don't understand each other.

"This reindeer finds ways to help families in need and encourages them daily.
I nominate a true leader. I nominate Reindeer Rosa."

A few whispers and murmurs, "Can Reindeer Rosa lead successfully?"

"A girl leader?" is heard in the auditorium.

Before Ms. Claus writes Rosa's name, several elves' hands go up.

"I have a concern," spoke Elf Katharine.

Everyone waits to hear what Elf Katharine has to say.

"We love Reindeer Rosa, but we need to know if her rose shaped nose will be a problem while she's leading the sleigh. She just looks different. Will her funny shaped nose make the other reindeer get off track?"

"Is her nose powerful enough to be the leader? Is it strong enough to light the way?" adds Gillian. "It only shines a slight pink glow. Is that really bright enough to lead the team?"

Poor Reindeer Rosa lowers her head in embarrassment. Her heart beats faster. Her face feels hot and sweaty, and her cheeks turn a bright pink like her rose shaped nose. She has never known this feeling.

"Can it be that others really think I look different? Why would they say something that makes me feel so sad?"

As she thinks about this, Reindeer Rosa reminds herself how important this vote really is. Somehow, even that thought doesn't make her feel better. She wants to run from the auditorium and hide. "I will never be able to look at anyone in Toyland again," she whispers to herself.

Santa quickly stands, takes the microphone, looks at Reindeer Rosa and smiles. "Rosa, I have known you all your life. I've watched you grow up. Rosa, I have been impressed with your gentleness, your caring spirit, your hard work, and your dependable nature. No matter what job you are given, you never argue or fuss. You do your very best with a good attitude.

"Everyone knows how hard you work. You always have time for others no matter how tired you are. You never complain. You feel great pride in every job you are given, regardless how small it may be. We often hear you singing as you work, putting everyone in a good mood.

"What a brilliant idea from our mayor to nominate you."

Santa pauses, taps his nose, thinks for a minute, and continues. "Rosa's nose reflects the beauty in all of us, and the soft, pink glow is just enough light to lead our team.

"Welcome to the team, Reindeer Rosa. You will make a wonderful leader!"

The soft glow of Rosa's nose shines brighter than ever, as she blushes at being in the spotlight.

Suddenly, everyone looks at Reindeer Rosa and sees more than her little, rose-shaped nose. "She really is beautiful," whispers Reindeer Freddy.

All eyes turn toward Reindeer Rosa. For the first time, everyone thinks about Reindeer Rosa's good qualities--her inner strength, kindness and goodness. Suddenly, they all see what a great leader Reindeer Rosa will be.

Elves and reindeer begin to clap and cheer their approval.

"It seems everyone votes yes on our nominees. We have our team for this year!" announces Mrs. Claus.

"Will the following reindeer please come to the front as your name is called?"

"We welcome this year's team:
Reindeer Marcelles,
Reindeer Joon,
Reindeer Juan Pablo, and
Reindeer Maurice.

"Let's hear it for Reindeer Claudia,
Reindeer Reyha
Reindeer Jin, and
Reindeer Malan.

"And now—last but not least-- the big announcement!
Leading our team is Reindeer Rosa."

Loud claps and cheers thunder all over the auditorium.

Santa laughs his big Ho, Ho, Ho. He gives each reindeer a warm, approving pat on the head to congratulate his new team members.

Santa hooks his thumbs in his belt, breathes a big sigh of relief and gives a quick wink to his sweetie, Mrs. Claus. Her heart is happy, as she smiles a smile meant only for Santa.

"Reindeer away!" Santa announces with a chuckle. He leads his grinning reindeer away to begin practicing as Santa's team for this year.

Suddenly, Santa stops at the door, and with a twinkle in his eye says, "All is well in Toyland."

Sleep tight, little ones. Santa will soon be on the way with lots of toys for all the good boys and girls. And wonder of wonders, Reindeer Rosa will lead the way with her calm, soft, pink glow."

"Merry Christmas everyone!"

"Shhhhhhh"

Reflection Questions

1) What is the main idea of this book? How do you support your answer?

2) Which character in the book, Santa's 911 Meeting, do you admire the most and why?

3) What are the characteristics of a good leader?

4) Tell about a time when you were a leader. How did it turn out?

5) What would you like to tell Rosa?

6) Always remember, you are a good leader. Have faith in yourself.

CPSIA information can be obtained at www.ICGtesting.com
Printed in the USA
LVOW02s1141161013

357147LV00001B/1/P